T0029376

save the . . .
PANDAS

by **Anita Sanchez**
with an introduction
by **Chelsea Clinton**

PHILOMEL

This is for you, Laine

PHILOMEL
An imprint of Penguin Random House LLC, New York

First published in the United States of America by Philomel,
an imprint of Penguin Random House LLC, 2024

Text copyright © 2024 by Chelsea Clinton

Photo credits: page 2: © Creativa Images/Adobe Stock; page 5: © Wandering Bear/Adobe
Stock; page 6: © Chansom Pantip/Adobe Stock; pages 11 and 22: © Cedar/Adobe Stock;
page 15: © wusuowei/Adobe Stock; page 19: leeyiutung/Adobe Stock; page 26: © Gary/
Adobe Stock; page 29: © Vadim Cebaniuc/Adobe Stock; page 35: © chintan patel/
Adobe Stock; page 41: © Pav-Pro/Adobe Stock; page 44: © AB Photography/Adobe Stock;
page 51: © NEWTRAVELDREAMS/Adobe Stock; page 55: © Kitch Bain/Adobe Stock;
page 63: © fotografie4you.eu/Adobe Stock; page 69: © aloha2014/Adobe Stock

Penguin supports copyright. Copyright fuels creativity, encourages diverse voices,
promotes free speech, and creates a vibrant culture. Thank you for buying an authorized
edition of this book and for complying with copyright laws by not reproducing, scanning,
or distributing any part of it in any form without permission. You are supporting writers
and allowing Penguin to continue to publish books for every reader.

Philomel is a registered trademark of Penguin Random House LLC.
The Penguin colophon is a registered trademark of Penguin Books Limited.

Visit us online at PenguinRandomHouse.com.

Library of Congress Cataloging-in-Publication Data is available.

ISBN 9780593623435 (hardcover)
ISBN 9780593623459 (paperback)

1st Printing

Printed in the United States of America

LSCC

Edited by Talia Benamy and Jill Santopolo • Design by Lily Qian
Text set in Calisto MT Pro

The publisher does not have any control over and does not assume any responsibility
for author or third-party websites or their content.

save the . . .

Dear Reader,

When I was around your age, my favorite animals were dinosaurs and elephants. I wanted to know everything I could about triceratopses, stegosauruses and other dinosaurs that had roamed our earth millions of years ago. Elephants, though, captured my curiosity and my heart. The more I learned about the largest animals on land today, the more I wanted to do to help keep them and other endangered species safe forever.

So I joined organizations working around the world to support endangered species and went to our local zoo to learn more about conservation efforts close to home (thanks to my parents and grandparents). I tried to learn as much as I could about how we can ensure animals and plants don't go extinct like the dinosaurs, especially since it's the choices that we're making that pose the greatest threat to their lives today.

The choices we make don't have to be huge to make

a real difference. When I was in elementary school, I used to cut up the plastic rings around six-packs of soda, glue them to brightly colored construction paper (purple was my favorite) and hand them out to whomever would take one in a one-girl campaign to raise awareness about the dangers that plastic six-pack rings posed to marine wildlife around the world. I learned about that from a book—*50 Simple Things Kids Can Do to Save the Earth*—which helped me understand that you're never too young to make a difference and that we all can change the world. I hope that this book will inform and inspire you to help save this and other endangered species. There are tens of thousands of species that are currently under threat, with more added every year. We have the power to save those species, and with your help, we can.

Sincerely,

Chelsea Clinton

save the . . .
PANDAS

CONTENTS

--- --- --- --- --- --- --- --- --- --- --- --- --- --- ---

1

A VERY RARE BEAR

Would you like to go to a panda's birthday party? You're invited!

The birthday boy is a roly-poly young panda named Xiao Qi Ji. His parents came from China, but he was born at the Smithsonian's National Zoo in Washington, DC. To celebrate his second birthday, the zoo staff made him his own special cake, a giant "fruitsicle" of frozen fruit juice, decorated with bananas and chunks of sweet potato, apple, and sugarcane. Visitors to the zoo watched as the cub eagerly licked his cake. They sang him a chorus of "Happy Birthday" and cheered him on as he gobbled a whole banana from the cake, peel and all. On YouTube and other social media sites, tens of thousands of panda fans also enjoyed this unusual birthday party.

Party with a panda!

The reason so many people are happy about Xiao Qi Ji's birthday is that pandas have been severely endangered for a long time. Every panda cub that's born is a win for the conservation of this magnificent species.

Bears in the Mist

Giant pandas are a species of bear. They're called giant pandas so that we don't confuse them with another kind of animal called a red panda, which is not closely related to the giant panda at all and is actually more like a raccoon. Pandas are endemic to China, which means that wild pandas live only in that one place and nowhere else in the world. They're found only in tiny, remote sections of China's Sichuan, Shaanxi, and Gansu provinces.

Xiao Qi Ji lives in a zoo. But in the wild,

pandas live in forests—forests of grass. It's a special kind of grass called bamboo, and it's very different from the grass you walk on. Imagine grass that grows past your knees, past your waist, and over your head. It keeps growing, towering high in the air, its thick woody stems clacking together and its narrow leaves rustling in the wind.

Now imagine a bear ambling slowly through the greenery—a vivid black-and-white body with big black eye patches on its round face. These beautiful animals spend their whole lives in those bamboo forests, which grow high in the mountains of China. They wander the steep slopes, living on hillsides and in valleys scattered with huge old evergreens and dense bamboo thickets. In spring and fall, chilly fog often fills the valleys. In winter, snow blankets

The green, misty mountains of China are where pandas roam.

the highest parts of the mountains. The bamboo growing on these rugged mountainsides is the pandas' only home—and their only food.

A Tasty Forest

Different kinds of bears like different kinds of foods. Some, like polar bears, eat almost nothing but meat. Grizzly bears are very fond of fish. Black bears, found across most of the

United States, eat all kinds of foods—they love insects, berries, and sweet, sticky honey. The panda is the only species of bear that eats almost nothing but plants. In the wild, 99 percent of a panda's diet is the leaves, stems, and shoots of bamboo plants. Every so often, if it happens to find one, a panda will eat a bug or a small rodent. But mostly it's all bamboo, all the time.

Pandas live in a forest of grass.

You'd think it would get boring eating the same food every single meal, every single day for your entire life. But pandas really seem to like eating bamboo. Even in a zoo, where there's a huge menu of food to pick from—pineapple, watermelon, lettuce, sweet sugarcane—pandas still mostly choose to munch their beloved bamboo. The chubby bears sit up on their rear ends like humans, holding long branches in their paws and steadily chewing their way through the crunchy stalks and leaves. Sometimes they peel the tough outer bark away from the stems, like you might peel a banana, and enjoy the crisp center.

Long ago, pandas were more like other bears and ate all sorts of things, including meat. But millions of years ago, that began to change. Scientists studying fossils of that long-ago time think that perhaps the kinds of animals that pandas hunted became rarer and rarer. So pandas began to seek out other sources of food. And there all around them were bamboo plants. Not only was bamboo plentiful and super easy to get, but also very few other creatures were eating it. Slowly, pandas developed into plant-eaters. There are many different species of bamboo. Arrow bamboo, with its slim, straight stems, is one of their favorites, and they also enjoy umbrella bamboo and golden bamboo.

But there are some problems with a diet of nothing but bamboo. Pandas still have a digestive system that's good at digesting meat, and they have a hard time getting enough nutrients from the bamboo they eat. This means that pandas have to eat a lot of it to get the protein, vitamins, and minerals they need to survive. Pandas eat for hours on end, packing away twenty to thirty pounds of bamboo a day. Having to eat a lot means having to poo a lot. Pandas poop many times throughout the day and night—forty times or more!

Bamboo may be easy to find, but it's not easy to eat. Like all grasses, it's made of tough, stringy fibers that are hard to digest. The stems are hard, woody, and difficult to chew. But pandas have evolved to cope with their favorite food. They have round heads and adorably plump cheeks—cute faces that are actually packed with power. Pandas have strong, heavy jaws and thick skulls to support powerful chewing muscles. Their front teeth are sharp for biting off leaves and shoots, and their back teeth, called molars, are large and flat for grinding tough bamboo stems. (Their teeth are a lot like yours in that way—sharper in the front and flatter in the back!)

If you reached out to pick a blade of grass, you'd use your thumb and a few fingers to grasp it. But pandas don't have thumbs! Like other bears, they have flat, doglike paws. A bone in their wrist, called the radial sesamoid bone, has developed to act like a short, fat thumb. This helps them to grip bamboo stems firmly as they efficiently strip leaves off.

Follow the Shoots

For a panda, it's not only how to eat bamboo, it's *when* to eat it. The earliest spring shoots of bamboo are much more nutritious than the fully grown stems. They're also easier to digest because they're softer. Pandas seem to know this by instinct, and they seek out the delicate green shoots early in the spring. Because temperatures are colder the higher into the mountains you climb, the first spring growth happens down in the warmer valleys.

In order to study how pandas can survive

Pandas' paws let them eat like people do.

while eating such a low-nutrition diet, a team of Australian scientists worked with the Chinese government. The researchers attached collars with GPS trackers to two pandas in the Foping National Nature Reserve, which is in the Qin Mountains of China. The GPS units showed exactly where the pandas were every three hours. As the seasons passed, the scientists kept track of where the pandas went and what they were eating.

The two hungry pandas started in the low-lands, eating young shoots rich in protein. But as the summer drew on, the shoots got leathery and harder to chew. So the pandas moved to higher ground, seeking fresh green shoots. The pandas would eat one kind of bamboo for a week or so and then switch to another kind. As time passed, the pandas ranged up and down the mountainsides, always seeking the young, tender growth.

Finding their favorite bamboo isn't just a matter of enjoying the taste—since bamboo is so low in nutritional value, it's vitally important for pandas to eat only the best. Pandas will climb high into trees to reach the most nutritious leaves. So climbing is a very important skill for pandas to have—but it turns out that some pandas are much better at it than others!

2

PANDA LIFE

Two baby pandas are climbing a tree. One of the babies is really good at making her way up the tree trunk. She grasps a branch with sharp claws, then quickly hoists herself up to the next branch. When she gets stuck, she arches her neck around the trunk and braces herself with her head to help her balance.

However, the other baby just can't seem to get the hang of it. She sits on a branch, thinks for a

Right: Not all pandas are good at climbing!

while, then reaches lazily for another branch, but it's too far to grab. Then she slides down to the ground, landing on her plump bottom. The cub rolls over and loses interest in climbing, wandering off to see what else there is to do.

Two wildlife researchers, Andrew Schulz and Rose Zhao, are watching the young pandas, carefully studying their movements. Both the babies were born in captivity at the Chengdu Research Base of Giant Panda Breeding in China. The staff is deciding which young pandas to release into the wild. The energetic climber is a likely candidate to be released, since she has a good chance of finding food and avoiding predators in the harsh conditions of the forest.

There are only about 1,800 pandas still living in the bamboo forests. Approximately six hundred more live in zoos or research centers, mostly in China. The pandas in captivity are very well taken care of. A big heap of fresh green bamboo is provided for each meal, along with treats of tasty fruit and sugarcane. Zoo nutritionists make special cookies filled with vitamins and minerals for the pandas to nibble. Veterinarians give the pandas regular health checkups. Zoo pandas can even go to a panda dentist if they need to.

So zoo life is easy—and safer. In the wild, cubs are sometimes threatened by predators such as wild dogs, leopards, or jackals. But in the safety of a zoo, panda cubs never have to risk becoming dinner, and the fun-loving babies often have lots of other cubs to hang out with, wrestling, roughhousing, snacking, and napping together.

In the bamboo forest, life is much harder.

The young pandas in the research center that are chosen for release will have a life of freedom, but it won't be a life of ease.

A Wild Life

Adult pandas spend most of their time eating, and they eat day and night. They munch for several hours and then nap for a while. Full-grown adult pandas are so big—they can weigh three hundred pounds—that they have no natural predators. So they don't need to climb trees or hide in a den to find a safe place to sleep. They just sprawl out wherever they happen to feel like it, snoozing on their bellies or relaxing on their backs. After a refreshing nap, they wake to eat again.

Wild pandas don't usually hang out in groups or spend a lot of time playing or socializing

Where does a panda nap? Wherever it wants to!

with each other. Scientists think that this may
be because their low-nutrient diet leaves them
little energy for anything besides looking for
food and eating it. Each panda has a home
area, called a range, of about five square miles.
If they bump into another panda, they're not
interested in making friends! The two will grunt,
swat, and bite at each other till one backs off
and goes away.

However, their loner lifestyle changes when

it's time for grown-up pandas to find a mate. This happens only during the short span of just a few days in the spring.

When it's time to mate, it's not easy for male and female pandas to spot each other in a forest dense with leaves and often shrouded in mist. Pandas don't see very well—in fact, anything more than five feet away probably just looks like a blur to them. The way for pandas to get together is to use their noses. Pandas have a super-keen sense of smell, and they can sniff out another panda even if it's more than a mile away. Boars (males) and sows (females) both follow scent clues to find mates.

Pandas looking for a mate will leave a message that's delivered loud and clear to another panda's nose. They do this by urinating. Panda pee contains many complex chemicals that have a strong, long-lasting odor. Boars will get so enthusiastic about leaving their smelly love letters that they'll spray their urine all over the side of a tree and even clamber up the trunk backward so as to leave the scent higher up on the bark. It looks like they're doing a handstand with their front paws on the ground and rear ends in the air! Both males and females also have a special organ called a scent gland underneath their tails. It's kind of like a small plastic bag filled with a waxy, sticky substance. The bears squeeze the smelly stuff onto rocks, logs, or tree trunks. Then they can use their fluffy tails like paintbrushes to spread the scent around.

Any panda that comes along will sniff at the scent marker. To a human nose, it would just have a stinky, skunky odor, but a panda nose can decode all sorts of information with a sniff—whether the other panda is male or female, how long ago they were there, and how healthy they are. A male can learn if there are other boars around and then avoid them. A female can learn how many possible mates are in the neighborhood. She can even tell how big the male is from how high up on the tree he's been able to get his urine, and sows tend to choose larger boars for their mates.

A panda checks out the latest news with his nose.

Pandas also "talk" to each other. But they don't give fearsome roars like most bears do. Instead, they make all kinds of weird sounds. Some panda noises are bearlike grunts and snorts, but pandas can also squeak and honk, or make sounds like a lamb bleating or a bird chirping. Using scent and sound, the pandas eventually find each other.

Big Mama, Little Baby

After mating, the male leaves and doesn't help raise the young—it's all up to Mom. She's pregnant for only a short time, between three and six months, which is a much shorter gestation period than other large mammals. Some scientists think it's because of their diet. The low nutrition in bamboo means a mother panda's body doesn't have a lot of nutrients left over to develop the bones, organs, and muscles of a large cub. So the baby panda is born before it's had time to develop eyes or ears, or grow any fur at all. It looks like a tiny pink blob about the size of a hamster and weighs about as much as a coffee mug. The mother is nine hundred times bigger than her baby!

Good thing the mighty mother is such an excellent caretaker. The mother and baby hang out in a cozy den in a cave or the trunk of a hollow tree. For the first few weeks, she keeps the helpless infant tucked in her thick, warm fur. The almost hairless baby can't stay warm without her, so she has to stay in the den without eating to guard the precious cub. In about a week, more hairs begin to sprout on the little body, but it can take many days before the baby has enough fur to keep warm on its own while the mother leaves the den to take a quick break to look for some food. She needs to eat even more than usual in order for her body to make milk for the growing cub.

For many months, the baby's only food is its mother's milk. A mother panda tenderly guides her cub to the nipples on her chest and nurses it often, cradling it like a human mother would. The baby doesn't open its eyes for six weeks and can barely move for the first three months.

As long as the mother gets enough nutrition to provide milk for the baby, the cub grows steadily. The panda baby is completely dependent on Mom, and it nurses for half a year or more. Eventually, the baby grows teeth and begins to nibble bamboo leaves. By watching Mom, the youngster learns how to be a panda: figuring out which kinds of bamboo are best and where to

Pandas have differently shaped eye patches that help them recognize each other.

find them, how to climb a tree, and when to nap. No longer is the baby pink and hairless— now it has beautiful black-and-white fur.

Black and White

Why are pandas such a vivid checkerboard of black and white? No one knows for sure. But it might be that their bold patchwork coloring helps them hide. The pandas' fur provides camouflage, helping the young bears hide from predators. It might seem as though the jet black and pure white would make the panda stand out instead of hiding it, but actually, if you're searching for a panda in the shadowy forest, they're surprisingly hard to find. The pandas blend into the patterns of sunshine, shade, and fog.

Unlike most kinds of bears, pandas don't hibernate, even though their mountainsides can be very cold and covered with snow in winter. Hibernating animals have to fatten up by eating lots of extra calories so that they can sleep without eating for many long months. But bamboo is the ultimate low-fat diet. So pandas can't sleep the winter away—they have to stay active to eat all winter long and often need to walk through snow. All-black fur would really make them easy to spot. But their black-and-white shapes are hard to see when the sun casts shadows on the snow. This helps the young cubs to hide from anything that might want to have them for dinner.

Panda Diplomacy

Pandas have long been regarded as very special animals by many Chinese people. Their black-and-white fur is a reminder of the ancient Chinese yin-yang symbol meaning harmony and balance. In an ancient Chinese history text called the *Shangshu*, which dates back more than two thousand years, pandas were described as strong and invincible, and over the centuries, pandas have been valued as bringers of good luck. To this day, the panda's friendly face appears on Chinese coins, bills, and postage stamps. A cheerful panda cartoon was the official mascot of the 2022 Olympic Games that were held in Beijing, the capital of China.

What does this ancient symbol of harmony and balance remind you of?

In the past, pandas were given as gifts by the Chinese people as a way of showing friendship to another nation, and today, they lend pandas to other countries for the same reason. This is known as panda diplomacy, and it's gone on for a very long time. According to tradition, a Chinese empress named Wu Zetian gave a pair of giant pandas to Japan more than two thousand years ago.

China gave the first pandas to the United States in 1941, and since then many other countries have been given these furry presents. In 1972, China gave the US another pair of pandas, named Hsing-Hsing and Ling-Ling, and received a gift in return—two huge, shaggy musk oxen from Alaska.

China has given pandas to many nations, and the plump, adorable bears immediately become stars of any zoo they are in. Not only are they magnificent to look at, they're also really fun to watch. They are curious and playful, love toys and puzzles, and are incredibly talented at doing somersaults. In zoos all over the world, from Australia to South Korea to the United Kingdom, millions of visitors watch the fascinating animals and become panda fans.

The Last Pandas

As panda diplomacy spread, so did pandas' fame, and soon they were the stars of cartoons and movies. Panda toys and teddy bears were cuddled by kids everywhere. But even as pandas became more and more popular, few people were aware that the number of pandas that remained in the wild forests of China was quickly shrinking.

In the 1980s, wildlife researchers studying pandas realized a terrible fact—there were only about a thousand of the animals left in the wild! In 1990, giant pandas were officially declared to be an endangered species—in grave danger of extinction.

What had happened? And how can we save the beautiful bears?

3

A SHRINKING FOREST

A panda ambles through gray mist that drifts through ferns and tall stalks of bamboo. Wind rustles the long, thin leaves and shakes water droplets from the dark green needles of spruce trees. From the branch of a gnarled pine, a golden snub-nosed monkey chatters and scolds, while in the topmost twigs, blackbirds and finches chirp. The panda strolls on, heading for her favorite patch of arrow bamboo. But she stops when she reaches a place where the trees come to a sudden end.

A newly built blacktop road stretches across her path. A distant roar gets louder and louder. She blinks in the glare as the bright headlights of a truck whiz by. Confused, the bear turns away from the noisy highway and heads back into the safety of the trees.

Pandas have roamed the land of China for millions of years. The cool, damp forests where bamboo thrives once spread over millions of square miles. The steep hillsides and river valleys were filled with many different species of bamboo, shaded by the big evergreen trees that make such cozy dens for panda mothers. No one knows exactly how many pandas there were long ago, but they probably numbered in the tens of thousands.

But in the 1950s, a big change began. China's

population grew by leaps and bounds, increasing from about 500 million people then to more than 1.4 billion people today. A billion more people meant that a lot more land was needed for houses, stores, and roads. Forests that had once been panda habitats were cut down, and the trees were turned into lumber and paper products. In many places, bustling towns filled with people replaced the acres of bamboo that once fed thousands of pandas.

As time went by, the forests got smaller and smaller. Roads and highways divided forests into ever-smaller chunks. As more and more people moved into panda territory, the shy bears moved out, climbing to areas where the land was too steep for houses or farms. Pandas clustered in six different remote mountainous areas, in small pockets of forest divided from each other by roads, railroad tracks, and towns.

Even though China began to create some reserves to protect pandas in 1957, it wasn't enough space for pandas to maintain a healthy

When the forest is cut down, where can the pandas go?

population. Logging continued until 80 percent of the forests that had made up panda habitats had been lost. Would the bamboo forest keep shrinking, chainsawed and bulldozed bit by bit, until it vanished forever?

Red Listed

An organization called the International Union for Conservation of Nature (IUCN) keeps a list called the IUCN Red List of Threatened Species™, which has all of the known endangered species in the whole world on it. There are seven categories to label species as threatened. Least Concern, Near Threatened, and Vulnerable mean the animals are mostly doing okay, but there's reason to be concerned about their future. When an animal is at risk of becoming extinct soon, it's listed as Endangered, or worse, Critically Endangered. Extinct in the Wild means the species doesn't exist anywhere outside zoos or research centers. The last category is the saddest: Extinct, which means the species is gone forever.

In the 1980s, panda numbers kept getting

smaller as the destruction of their habitat continued. It was clear they were in desperate need of help. In 1990, the IUCN placed giant pandas on the Red List as an Endangered species.

But an Endangered status meant that there was still time to save the pandas.

In 1979, China's National Forestry and Grassland Administration began working with a not-for-profit organization called the World Wildlife Fund (WWF) to make a plan to save the pandas. An important part of the plan was to create more panda reserves: places where the forests would be protected and people would not move in and build houses or farms. But it turns out that finding the best places for panda reserves isn't easy. One problem is that the bamboo forest is a place of constant change.

Here Today, Gone Tomorrow

A bamboo forest is a very different place from a forest of trees. Oaks, spruces, and pines are plants that can grow in the same places for hundreds of years. Their leaves or seeds would provide a constant supply of food for wildlife. But remember that bamboo isn't a tree; it's a type of grass.

There are more than a thousand different species of bamboo, but pandas will only eat a few of those. And even if there are many acres of lush green shoots and leaves, sometimes pandas go hungry. That's because bamboo plants have a very strange lifestyle.

A huge area of bamboo will grow for a while, maybe twenty years or even more. Then, all at once, every single one of the bamboo plants of that species burst into flower, and then they all wither away and die! No more leaves or fresh shoots—nothing but dead stalks. It will often take ten years or more before that area of bamboo has regrown enough to be a food source.

So there has to be more than one species of bamboo in a panda reserve. Pandas need to have other bamboo supplies always available to eat. If all the bamboo has died off, they have to migrate to a different area—and that's not always easy.

In the days when bamboo grew for millions of square miles, pandas could always find a new source of food. But the small remaining sections of habitat are cut off from each other like islands. A panda population could face starvation if all the bamboo dies off at once and they can't reach fresh supplies.

A Nice Warm Tree

Another problem is that pandas need shelter as well as food. While taking care of their tiny, furless babies, panda mothers must have a snug, dry den. They need to keep their young warm and protected from the rain and cold of the Chinese mountainsides. Pandas will den in caves, but they seem to like hollow trees better.

To find out why, Chinese and American scientists worked together on a field study in old-growth forests, which are forests that have been growing for a century or more without being logged or greatly disturbed by people. In Fengtongzhai National Nature Reserve, they searched for rocky caves that could be possible dens and for big trees that had hollows large enough for denning. Then they carefully measured the temperature and humidity inside both

Pandas need big trees in their habitat.

types of places and discovered what panda moms knew all along—big hollow tree trunks are much cozier than caves. Caves are hotter in summer and colder and damper in winter. The thick trunk of an old pine tree will keep a constant, comfortable temperature inside the den.

But it takes a tree a long, long time to grow big enough to shelter a two-hundred-pound mama and her baby. The best den trees are found in old-growth forests.

So for a place to be a good home for giant pandas, it needs several different species of bamboo as well as old-growth forests with plenty of den trees. It also has to be big enough that adult pandas can spread out and have enough room to roam.

Perfect panda habitat is very hard to find because there's not a lot of land left that meets all of a panda's needs. The Chinese government has created some panda reserves on open land that used to be farms. Even though new bamboo is being planted, these areas aren't as good for pandas as the reserves that protect old-growth forests.

Heating Up

With their thick fur, adult pandas thrive in their chilly mountain homes. They don't mind cloudy, wet weather, and they love to frolic in the snow. But pandas can't cope with heat. The big furry bears get dehydrated easily, which means their bodies need water. If they get too overheated, they can even die.

Pandas' favorite food plant has the same problem. The kinds of bamboo that pandas need to eat can only grow in a cool climate. A bit of snow doesn't bother it, but it dies off if the temperature gets too hot.

And our world is warming. Human-caused pollution—by things like cars, power plants, and factories giving off carbon dioxide and other gases—has changed Earth's atmosphere. One of the biggest threats to our planet is climate change caused by these gases, which trap the sun's heat and keep it close to Earth. The effects of climate change are being felt all over the world.

Pandas are looking to us for support.

In the pandas' habitats, this is bad news for the bamboo that grows down in the warmer valleys. That bamboo is dying off as temperatures rise, and bamboo is growing higher up the mountains than it used to. Pandas are having to travel farther uphill to find their food. But what happens when the pandas and their food plants reach the tops of the mountains and there's nowhere cooler to go? Scientists are just beginning to study ways to help pandas survive the challenges of climate change.

What's Next?

Thanks to panda researchers who spend months and years in the remote mountains of China, we're starting to understand pandas' problems and what they need to survive. Scientists all over the world are working to create a plan to help pandas come back from the edge of extinction.

And they've discovered that one way to help the pandas is to have more panda birthday parties!

4

MANY HAPPY RETURNS

On a summer evening in August 2020, a female panda named Mei Xiang curled herself up in her cozy den. She knew it was time for her baby to arrive. When the tiny infant was born, she cuddled him close and gave him a nice, warm bath with her tongue. Then he snuggled closer and began to nurse.

But Mei Xiang's den wasn't in a hollow tree on a misty Chinese mountainside. She was curled in a snug, closet-sized room padded with soft straw in the Smithsonian's National Zoo. Video cameras on the walls allowed veterinarians, nutritionists, and other zoo staff to watch the mother's every movement. If she had any trouble giving birth or caring for her baby, they were ready to help. But Mei Xiang was twenty-two years old, which is fairly old for a panda, and this was her fourth cub, so she was a very experienced mom. Her cub was soon growing strong and healthy.

Three months after this happy birthday, the zoo invited the public to suggest names for the new baby. The winning name was Xiao Qi Ji, which means "little miracle" in Mandarin Chinese. And it truly is a miracle that this baby and many other panda babies are helping bring their species back from the brink of extinction as part of a program of breeding pandas in zoos.

Bottle-Fed Pandas

Why is it so important that pandas have babies in zoos? If the animals are given a protected habitat that meets their needs, can't we just leave them alone to take care of themselves?

Pandas are going to have a hard time surviving without the help of people—at least for a while. Giant pandas have a very low rate of reproduction (which means they don't have very many babies that quickly). A mother mouse, for instance, can give birth at only six weeks old and can have a litter of six babies once a month! But a panda mom doesn't have her first baby till she's about four or five years old. She spends a year and a half or more taking care of a single cub. Panda mothers often have twins, but they just don't produce enough milk to feed two babies. The mother

study what a newborn panda needs. Chinese scientists worked with staff from the San Diego Zoo Wildlife Alliance and other zoos and research centers to help baby pandas survive.

First, the San Diego Zoo's experts in nutrition invented a baby formula for pandas. Their own mother's milk is best for newborns, but panda moms, especially if they are first-time mothers, sometimes have trouble making sure the babies get all the milk they need. The formula the experts created was filled with vitamins and minerals and was tasty enough that the babies would drink it. Researchers experimented till they found just the right size and shape for a tiny nipple to fit into little panda mouths. That way zookeepers could bottle-feed the infants and make sure they got plenty of nutrition.

Then, Chinese zoo staff at the Wolong Panda

Center came up with the idea of twin swapping. If a mother had twins, the zookeepers could quietly remove one newborn twin from the den and bottle-feed it. Then they would sneakily switch the babies in between the mother's feeds. That way, each baby would get a mixture of some of its mother's milk and some formula. And, like human babies, newborn pandas need lots of cuddling. Zookeepers would snuggle

Zookeepers take good care of their babies.

with the infants and keep them warm until it was time to switch again.

One of the main places where pandas are bred is the Chengdu Research Base of Giant Panda Breeding in China. In 1987, wildlife biologists rescued six pandas from the forest that were sick and weak from starvation. The pandas were nursed back to health, and soon they were mating and producing healthy babies. By 2020, there were more than two hundred healthy giant pandas, all descendants of the original six.

It took years of research, but zookeepers got better and better at helping the little pink, hairless cubs survive. Today, their success rate is more than 90 percent.

It's great that there are more and more panda birthdays every year. But the point of breeding pandas in zoos is not to have more animals in cages for people to look at. It's to create a healthy population that can thrive in the wild. So the question is how to turn cuddly zoo babies into wild animals.

The first step is to dress up in a panda suit.

Back to Nature

Just like human babies, panda babies form a strong bond with the one who cuddles and feeds them. If the panda is going to spend its life in a zoo, then it's important to build that bond of trust with the people on the zoo staff so that they can help if the animal is sick or injured. If the panda needs medicine or help with birth, it won't be overly stressed by having humans get close. But if the panda is going to be released into the wild, it's not good for it to be depending on humans.

At the Wolong Panda Center in China, the zookeepers often dress up in panda costumes. They might look like they're ready for trick-or-treating, but they don't care if they look silly. They know it's important to pretend to be pandas when they care for the babies that are scheduled to be released into the wild. That way, the babies won't come running for treats every time they see a human in the forest.

Don't forget that pandas depend on their noses a lot. The zookeepers also have to smell like pandas! They rub panda urine or droppings on their costumes to make sure that the youngsters get used to panda scent instead of people smell.

You can't release a panda cub into the forest until it can feed and take care of itself. In the wild, a baby learns from watching its mother and copying what she does. But if Mom has never been in the wild herself, she can't teach her baby everything it needs to know to face the challenges of the world outside.

For a captive-born cub, it's not easy to learn how to be a wild panda. The first time a release was tried, the young panda died after just ten

The wild forest is a tough place for young pandas.

months. After that, scientists spent years re-searching how to prepare the animals before they tried again.

Learning to Be a Panda

As soon as little Zhang Xiang was born, the staff at Wolong had high hopes for her. They planned for her to be one of the first pandas released into the wild—because she had a teacher that knew what had to be learned. Her mother, Zhang Ka, was born in the wild and rescued as a young adult when she became ill. Having lived in the wild for years, this mom knew the hard lessons that wild pandas have to learn.

Zhang Xiang didn't grow up in a cage. Soon after her birth, she and her mother were placed in a huge enclosure as big as thirty soccer fields and filled with bamboo plants, trees, and a water hole. Zhang Ka gave her baby lessons in tree climbing, bamboo finding, and den choosing. The animals were watched constantly on video cameras but rarely saw humans, and then only if they were wearing panda suits.

Once Zhang Xiang had proved she was strong, smart, and good at climbing trees, she had to pass another test. The Wolong staff put a stuffed leopard in the enclosure, rubbed it with leopard urine to make it smell like a live predator, and played recorded growls. If Zhang Xiang had approached and curiously sniffed the dummy leopard, she would have failed the test. A friendly, confident panda would have a hard time making it in the wild—only the cautious and wary can survive. Perhaps the little panda was well-named—Zhang Xiang means "the thoughtful one." She passed the test by carefully avoiding the scary leopard.

Young pandas usually leave their mothers at two years old. So just after her second birthday, Zhang Xiang was placed in a small cage and taken to Liziping National Nature Reserve, which has a tiny population of about a dozen pandas. When the cage door was opened, she strolled out and sniffed her new home. A photographer, who was dressed up in a tree costume to avoid scaring her, took photos as the young panda disappeared into the forest.

Would she survive?

For a long time, little was known about how she was doing. Then, four years after her release, she reappeared far from where she had started. A remote camera revealed that the cub had traveled to Yele Nature Reserve many miles away. The film showed Zhang Xiang sniffing at a male scent marker on a tree trunk. Perhaps she was in the process of finding a mate.

Reintroducing pandas into wild habitats is a slow and painstaking process. So far only about a dozen pandas have successfully been released. But as researchers learn more, the rate of survival gets better and gives more hope for the giant panda's future.

Places for Pandas

The people of China are working hard to protect their pandas. The Chinese government has created dozens of panda reserves, which cover almost four million acres of forest. In 1998, China banned logging in most areas where pandas live. The Chinese are also working on making connections between pockets of forests by planting long strips of bamboo between them to create corridors, or pathways. Now pandas can follow a narrow path of green to explore new places. They can find more food supplies and meet new pandas to mate with.

Pandas are also strictly protected by Chinese law. In the past, giant pandas were sometimes hunted for their thick, rich fur. Panda pelts, or skins, used to be highly prized for their luxurious warmth and soft beauty. Just one panda pelt could sell for thousands of dollars. But for many years, all hunting of pandas has been illegal, and poaching (hunting that's against the law) is punished by very severe penalties including long prison sentences.

These steps are helping pandas fight their way back from the edge of extinction. From only a thousand bears in 1980, their numbers have grown steadily. In 2021, China's Ministry of Ecology and Environment announced that the population of wild giant pandas had increased to more than 1,800. On the Red List, pandas were downlisted, meaning their category officially changed. Instead of being Endangered, giant pandas are now classified as the less worrying Vulnerable. That means they're not out of danger yet, but they're in much better shape to survive.

All of this is good news for pandas—and for millions of panda fans around the world!

Umbrella Species

Taking care of pandas and creating panda reserves is a very, very expensive process. The government of China has poured more than a billion dollars into breeding and reintroduction programs. Other countries and not-for-profit organizations have also spent hundreds of millions of dollars protecting pandas and their habitat. And some might wonder—is it really worthwhile to focus so much time and attention and resources on just one single species? Why do pandas get all the love? So many other animals need our help!

Well, it turns out that giant pandas aren't the only creatures that hang out in the bamboo forest. Have you ever heard of a white-lipped deer? How about a fire-bellied toad? A dwarf blue sheep, a golden monkey, or a clouded leopard? All these species and thousands more live there, too—not just mammals, reptiles, birds, and amphibians but plants as well, including wild magnolia trees with huge milk-white flowers and rare orchids, mosses, and

Saving the bamboo forest helps save the rare clouded leopard, too.

ferns. When a panda habitat is protected, it creates a home for countless other species.

It's hard to raise money for a species that no one has ever heard of. But pandas are famous all over the world. And they're just so incredibly cute! Pandas' fame has helped the WWF, zoos, and other organizations receive enormous amounts of donations. Giant pandas are what biologists call an umbrella species. That's a species that lives in a habitat filled with other rare plants and animals, so protecting the umbrella species also protects many other species.

And it's not only wild plants and animals that shelter under the panda's umbrella. The mountains where the pandas live are filled with streams of clean, pure water. These flow down into the country's two main rivers, the Yangtze River and the Yellow River. By creating reserves to protect pandas, the water supply for humans is protected, too.

The Chinese government is giving rewards and tax breaks to farmers who plant fields of bamboo. This is good for pandas, but it's also great for the air we all breathe. Plants make their own food, and as they do, they absorb carbon dioxide from the air. Bamboo, a fast-growing plant, is especially good at absorbing carbon dioxide, which helps to lessen the effects of climate change.

By working to save the pandas, we're saving so much more . . . including ourselves.

Party for Pandas

Most of us live very far away from the misty mountainsides where pandas hang out. So what can we do to help? How can we stretch out a hand to help pandas when they're so far out of our reach?

Let's take a look at another panda birthday party. This one was for Ella, but she's not a panda, she's a ten-year-old human. Ella loves pandas, and she decided to share her birthday with her favorite animals. She invited friends and family to bring donations to her panda birthday party in return for goodie bags with panda stickers and treats. Her panda party raised $325.

Another panda fan named Ezra started helping pandas when he was six, selling drawings as notecards at a craft fair. So far, he's donated eighty dollars to help pandas. Third- and fourth-grade students at Oceanside Elementary School had a craft sale and lemonade stand that raised $235 for pandas. Another school helps their favorite bears at their annual Popcorn for Pandas sale.

Imagine how all those donations can help. Even a few dollars can buy a bottle of formula for a baby panda. Or purchase seeds for bamboo plantings. Or buy toys for young pandas in zoos. It takes about sixty dollars to buy a waterproof suit for a panda ranger who patrols a rainy panda reserve. About one hundred dollars could buy an energy-saving stove for a family so that they won't have to use so much firewood, which saves trees from being logged.

A quarter for a cookie, fifty cents for lemonade—it may not seem like enough to do any good. But when donations from young people all over the world are put together, it can really add up.

A Future for Pandas

When the birthday panda cub Xiao Qi Ji turns three years old, he will go home—to a land he's never seen.

Most of the pandas in zoos worldwide do

not belong to the country they're in. The animals are on loan from China, and they are eventually returned. When he goes back to his homeland, Xiao Qi Ji will be too old to be released into the wild. He will probably live at Wolong or another panda research center that is open to the public. Thousands of visitors from countries all over the world will admire his black-and-white beauty and laugh at his tricks and somersaults. And perhaps one day, some of his sons and daughters will be released to roam the wild bamboo forests.

There's still a lot we need to do to ensure a future for Xiao Qi Ji and his kind. But with so many people working to help them, we can hope for many more happy panda birthdays in the future.

Hoping for many more panda birthdays!

BLACK-AND-WHITE FACTS ABOUT PANDAS

1. Giant pandas don't all look alike! The black patches are different shapes on each animal. Researchers can identify the bears by using the shape of their eye patches. These differences may help pandas recognize each other, too.

2. There have been a few rare brown-and-white pandas.

3. The Mandarin Chinese word for giant panda is *dà xióng māo*, which means "giant bear cat."

4. In Chinese, repeating a name is a sign of

affection. That's why so many pandas are given names like Ling Ling or Tan Tan.

5. When eating, pandas usually sit on their bottoms and hold food with their paws. Pandas have specially adapted paws and can hold an apple and munch it like people do.

6. Pandas are very flexible and can get themselves into all sorts of yoga-like positions. They can even do floppy somersaults.

7. A special thick lining in pandas' throats and stomachs protects them from sharp bamboo splinters.

8. Pandas can stand up straight, but they don't usually walk upright. They don't swim very often, but they can swim well if they have to.

9. In a zoo, one of a panda's favorite cooldowns is to play with a big heap of ice cubes.

10. Pandas are zoo stars, and social media stars, too. The video of a Smithsonian's National Zoo panda named Tian Tian sliding in the snow during a blizzard has been viewed on social media millions of times.

11. Xin Xing, the oldest known giant panda, celebrated her thirty-eighth birthday at Chongqing Zoo. Like Xiao Qi Ji, she enjoyed a fruitsicle cake—hers had extra watermelon.

HOW YOU CAN HELP SAVE THE PANDAS

If you care about these beautiful bears, here are some ways you can become an activist in the fight to save them!

1. The more people who fall in love with pandas, the more people who will work to save them. Spread the word about pandas and what they need. Do a science fair project, start a school club, or work with a scout troop or youth organization. Consider working with adults to use social media.

2. Get to know pandas up close and personal so you can share your knowledge with others. You can watch the Smithsonian's National Zoo pandas any time on their live Giant Panda Cam at NationalZoo.si.edu/Webcams/Panda-Cam.

3. Use the power of art to raise awareness of the pandas' plight. Draw, paint, photograph, sew, write, dance, or sing about pandas and how amazing they are.

4. Brainstorm creative ways to raise money for pandas. Bake sales, raffles, and lemonade stands are great places to start. What else can you think of? Here are some organizations that can use the money you raise as donations to help pandas:

- Pandas International: PandasInternational.org/Pennies -4-Pandas
- World Wildlife Fund: WorldWildlife .org
- San Diego Zoo Wildlife Alliance: SanDiegoZooWildlifeAlliance.org

5. Have a panda party on International Giant Panda Day, celebrated around the world on March 16.

6. Buy better bamboo. Many things we buy are made of strong, lightweight bamboo wood: lawn chairs, cutting boards, fishing poles, musical instruments, picture frames. But was the bamboo you're buying logged from a wildlife habitat? Shop for wood products certified by the Forest Stewardship Council (FSC), a not-for-profit organization that works to protect forests.

7. Adopt a panda. No, you can't take one home, but you or your class could symbolically adopt a panda. After paying an adoption fee, you receive photos and information on how "your" panda is doing. You can do that through a number of organizations, including these:

- Pandas International: Store.PandasInternational.org /Symbolic-Adoptions
- World Wildlife Fund: Gifts.WorldWildlife.org/Gift-Center
- National Wildlife Federation: ShopNWF.org/Category/Shop -Adoption-Center-Adopt-an -Animal-Adopt-a-Giant-Panda

8. Is there a panda in your future? If working to protect wildlife is your hobby, maybe it could become your job! Research ways to pursue a career helping wildlife. Here are some places to start:

- The Wildlife Society: Wildlife.org /Wildlife-Careers
- LiveAbout: LiveAbout.com/Careers -with-Wildlife-125918
- National Wildlife Federation: NWF.org/About-Us/Careers

9. Write to your congressperson. Your representatives need to know what you think. Make it clear that you want them to take strong action to protect endangered species, especially pandas. Their contact info is available online at Congress.gov /Members/Find-Your-Member. If no one ever bothers to write or call about endangered species, what message does that send?

10. VOTE! One of the most important things anyone can do to help endangered species is to vote. Register to vote as soon as you can and support political candidates who support environmental and endangered species protection. Encourage those in your family of voting age to cast their ballot with the environment (and pandas!) in mind.

ACKNOWLEDGMENTS

Thanks to all the panda lovers, in China and all over the world, who are working to help save the pandas.

REFERENCES

Pandas International. "Pennies 4 Pandas." Accessed May 3, 2023. pandasinternational.org/pennies -4-pandas.

Reissman, Hailey. "Gallery: the School Where Pandas Learn How to Be Wild." *Ideas* (blog), TED, April 14, 2017. Accessed May 3, 2023. ideas.ted.com/gallery-the-school-where-pandas -learn-how-to-be-wild.

Ryder, Joanne and Katherine Feng. *Panda Kindergarten*. New York: HarperCollins, 2009.

San Diego Zoo Wildlife Alliance: Animals and

Plants. "Giant Panda." Accessed May 3, 2023.
animals.sandiegozoo.org/animals/giant-panda.

Schaller, George B. *The Last Panda.* Chicago:
University of Chicago Press, 1993.

Smithsonian's National Zoo and Conservation
Biology Institute. "Giant Panda." Accessed
May 3, 2023. nationalzoo.si.edu/animals
/giant-panda.

Thimmesh, Catherine. *Camp Panda: Helping Cubs
Return to the Wild.* Boston: Houghton Mifflin
Harcourt, 2018.

Vitale, Ami. *Panda Love: The Secret Lives of Pandas.*
London: Hardie Grant, 2018.

World Wildlife Fund. "Giant Panda." worldwildlife
.org/species/giant-panda.

ANITA SANCHEZ is especially fascinated by plants and animals that no one loves, and the unusual, often ignored wild places of the world. Her award-winning books sing the praises of the unappreciated: dandelions, poison ivy, tarantulas, mud puddles. Her goal is to make young readers excited about science and nature. Many years of fieldwork and teaching outdoor classes have given her firsthand experience in introducing students to the wonders of the natural world.

Photo by George Steele

You can visit Anita Sanchez online at
AnitaSanchez.com
and follow her on Twitter
@ASanchezAuthor

CHELSEA CLINTON is the author of the #1 *New York Times* bestseller *She Persisted: 13 American Women Who Changed the World*; *She Persisted Around the World: 13 Women Who Changed History*; *She Persisted in Sports: American Olympians Who Changed the Game*; *She Persisted in Science: Brilliant Women Who Made a Difference*; *Don't Let Them Disappear: 12 Endangered Species Across the Globe*; *Welcome to the Big Kids Club*; *It's Your World: Get Informed, Get Inspired & Get Going!*; *Start Now!: You Can Make a Difference*; with Hillary Clinton, *Grandma's Gardens* and *The Book of Gutsy Women: Favorite Stories of Courage and Resilience*; and, with Devi Sridhar, *Governing Global Health: Who Runs the World and Why?* She is also the Vice Chair of the Clinton Foundation, where she works on many initiatives, including those that help empower the next generation of leaders. She lives in New York City with her husband, Marc, and their children.

Photo courtesy of the author

You can follow Chelsea Clinton on Twitter
@ChelseaClinton
or on Facebook at
Facebook.com/ChelseaClinton

DON'T MISS MORE BOOKS IN THE

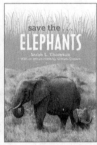

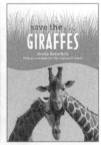

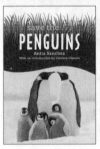

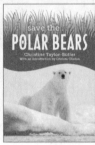

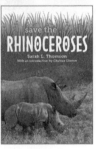

save the . . . SERIES!

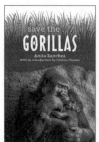

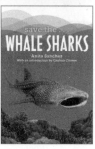